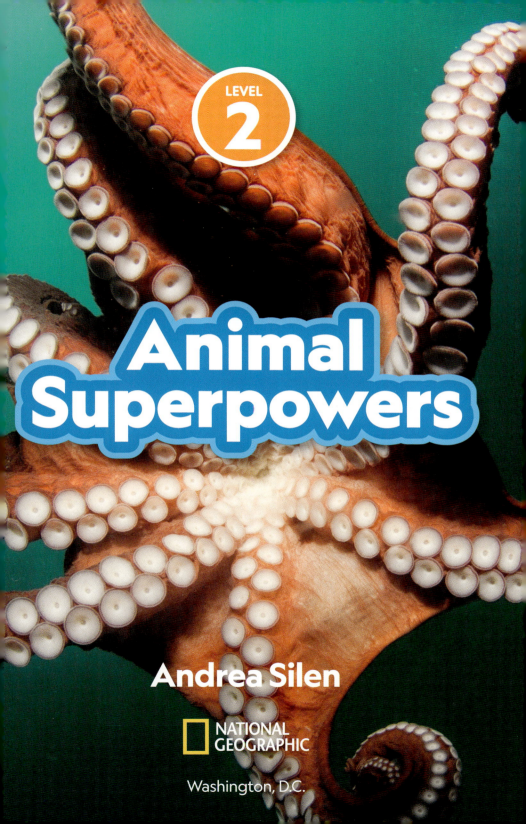

LEVEL 2

Animal Superpowers

Andrea Silen

NATIONAL GEOGRAPHIC

Washington, D.C.

To Edith and Jim —A.S.

Published by National Geographic Partners, LLC, Washington, DC 20036.

Copyright © 2023 National Geographic Partners, LLC. All rights reserved. Reproduction of the whole or any part of the contents without written permission from the publisher is prohibited.

NATIONAL GEOGRAPHIC and Yellow Border Design are trademarks of the National Geographic Society, used under license.

Designed by Anne LeongSon

The author and publisher gratefully acknowledge the fact-checking review of this book by Robin Palmer, as well as the literacy review of this book by Mariam Jean Dreher, professor emerita of reading education, University of Maryland, College Park.

Library of Congress Cataloging-in-Publication Data

Names: Silen, Andrea, author.
Title: Animal superpowers / Andrea Silen.
Description: Washington, D.C. : National Geographic, 2023. | Series: National geographic readers | Audience: Ages 5-8 | Audience: Grades 2-3
Identifiers: LCCN 2021019589 (print) | LCCN 2021019590 (ebook) | ISBN 9781426339776 (paperback) | ISBN 9781426339783 (library binding) | ISBN 9781426339790 (ebook) | ISBN 9781426339806 (ebook other)
Subjects: LCSH: Animal behavior--Juvenile literature.
Classification: LCC QL751.5 .S5525 2022 (print) | LCC QL751.5 (ebook) | DDC 591.5--dc23
LC record available at https://lccn.loc.gov/2021019589
LC ebook record available at https://lccn.loc.gov/2021019590

Photo Credits
AL = Alamy Stock Photo; AS = Adobe Stock; SS = Shutterstock
Cover, Nicholas Bergkessel, Jr./Science Source; 1, Konstantin Novikov/SS; 3, ftlaudgirl/AS; 4-5, Stephen Dalton/Nature Picture Library/AL; 6-7, Nature and Science/AL; 8-9, Gudkov Andrey/SS; 9 (UP), Joel Sartore/National Geographic Image Collection; 10-11, Kevin Wells Photography/SS; 12, Anaspides Photography - Iain D. Williams/AL; 13 (LO), Armelle Llobet/Getty Images; 14 (LO), Rasmus Loeth Petersen/AL; 14 (RT), Horizon International Images Limited/AL; 15, kaschibo/SS; 16 (UP), Dale Sutton/AL; 16 (RT), Ingo Rechenberg; 16 (LO), Michael Benard/SS; 17 (UP), Audrey Snider-Bell/SS; 17 (RT), blickwinkel/AL; 17 (LO), blickwinkel/AL; 19, ftlaudgirl/AS; 20, Andrei/AS; 21 (LE), Tim Krynak; 21 (RT), Tim Krynak; 22, WaterFrame/AL; 23, Paul Souders/Getty Images; 24-25, MMCez/SS; 26-27, Hummingbird Art/AS; 27, Tim Laman/Nature Picture Library/AL; 28-29, Ken Jones/Courtesy of University of Toronto Scarborough; 30 (UP), Cathy Keifer/SS; 30 (LO CTR), Abigail Barhorst/SS; 30 (LE), Unique Photo Arts/FOAP/Getty Images; 30 (LO RT), Horizon International Images Limited/AL; 30, Anaspides Photography - Iain D. Williams/AL; 30 (LO LE), Kevin Wells Photography/SS; 31 (UP), Audrey Snider-Bell/SS; 31 (RT), EdBrown/SS; 31 (LE), pclark2/AS; 31 (LO), Dancestrokes/SS; 32 (LO RT), Tim Krynak; 32 (UP RT), Tim Laman/Nature Picture Library/AL; 32 (UP LE), Bass Supakit/SS; 32 (LE), Elana Erasmus/SS; 32 (RT), Elana Erasmus/SS; 32 (LO LE), iPiCfootage.com/SS

Printed in the United States of America
23/WOR/1

Contents

Super Animals!	4
Amazing Speed!	6
Epic Strength!	10
Poof!	14
6 Amazing Spider Skills	16
Shape-Shifters!	18
Fighting Powers!	22
Super Senses!	24
Saving the Day!	28
Quiz Whiz	30
Glossary	32

Super Animals!

It's a bird that packs a punch! It's a spider that leaps great distances! It's a seahorse that's invisible to other animals!

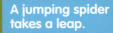
A jumping spider takes a leap.

Some critters have such amazing skills, they almost seem like superheroes. But these abilities are not just for show. They help the animals survive. Let's find out how!

Amazing Speed!

Some creatures move very quickly. Take the American pronghorn, for example.

Pronghorns are the fastest land mammals in North America.

At top speed, it can run nearly 60 miles an hour.

That's the speed many cars can go on the highway! Running fast helps the animal avoid predators.

Word Power

PREDATOR: An animal that hunts and eats other animals

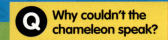
Q Why couldn't the chameleon speak?

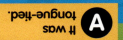
A It was tongue-tied.

Talk about fast food! Chameleons shoot out their tongues to snag yummy insects. They must act fast before the bugs get away. It takes them less than one second to grab lunch.

A chameleon's tongue can stretch to about twice the length of its body.

Brazilian free-tailed bats

Brazilian free-tailed bats soar around looking for snacks. They can fly up to 99 miles an hour. Some of the fastest pitchers can hurl a baseball at about the same speed.

Epic Strength!

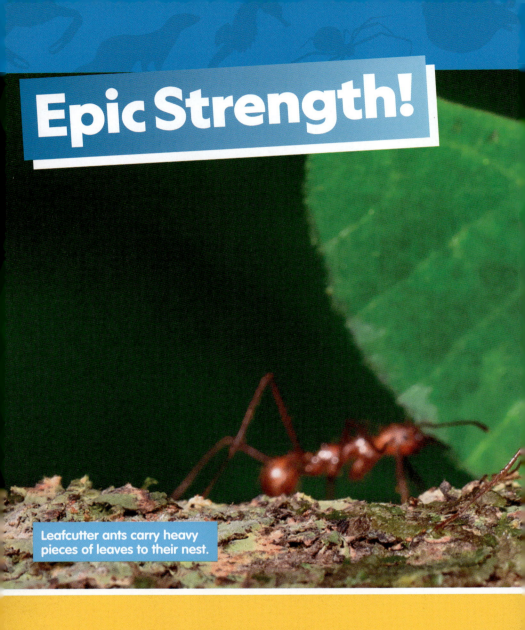

Leafcutter ants carry heavy pieces of leaves to their nest.

Superstrong animals are often big and have lots of muscles. But some are small and slim, like leafcutter ants.

One leafcutter ant can carry almost 50 times its own weight. That's like a human lifting a pickup truck!

Sea otters eat about one quarter of their body weight in food every day.

Crunch! Sea otters have powerful jaws. And their teeth are more than twice as strong as a human's. They use their mighty mouths to crack open hard clamshells to get to the meat inside.

Secretary birds snack on snakes. When they see one, they give it a big kick. The kick is so strong, it knocks their prey out cold.

Word Power

PREY: An animal that is eaten by another animal

A secretary bird winds up to deliver a powerful kick.

Poof!

Some creatures use camouflage (KAM-uh-flazh) to disappear from view. Cuttlefish change color at will. They may turn gray like rocks, green like seaweed, or many other colors.

Cuttlefish blend in with their surroundings to hide from predators.

Q What did the seahorse say when offered an apple? **A** "Nay!"

Pygmy (PIG-mee) seahorses are slow swimmers. But they have a special power to stay safe. Adults look bumpy and colorful just like their coral home. This makes them hard to spot.

Can you spot the seahorse?

Word Power

CAMOUFLAGE: An animal's natural color or shape that blends in with its surroundings

6 AMAZING Spider Skills

1

A common jumping spider can **leap 50 times its body length.** That's like a human jumping the length of a football field from one end line to the other.

2

Many fishing spiders can **walk on water.**

3

When threatened, Moroccan flic-flac spiders do **cartwheels** to get away.

4 Some tarantulas **throw** their **sharp leg hairs** at **enemies.**

5 Diving bell spiders **live underwater.** They create a **home** out of **webbing** and **air bubbles.**

6 One type of jumping spider **looks and acts** like an **ant** to **fool predators.**

17

Shape-Shifters!

A few animals can change their bodies in wacky ways. Pufferfish have stretchy stomachs. When threatened, they gulp water to make their bellies swell. Most pufferfish are also covered in spines that stick out when they swell. These changes make it harder for predators to eat them.

Some pufferfish can get as big as a beach ball!

A giant Pacific octopus can squeeze into tight spaces to find food.

A giant Pacific octopus can be longer than a car. But its soft body has no bones. It can wriggle through a hole that's only an inch wide!

Q What's a frog's favorite game? **A** Hopscotch.

The mutable (MEW-tuh-bull) rainfrog changes the texture (TEKS-chur) of its skin. It can go from smooth to spiky and back again. This may help it blend into its surroundings.

spiky

smooth

Word Power

TEXTURE: The way a surface feels and looks

Fighting Powers!

These creatures are ready for battle! Pom-pom crabs always carry a sea anemone (uh-NEM-uh-nee) in each claw. When they feel threatened, pom-pom crabs use these stinging sea animals to fend off predators.

Pom-pom crabs are also called boxer crabs.

Q How do you introduce yourself to a porcupine? **A** Very carefully.

A porcupine's quills can be a foot long.

The African crested porcupine is covered in quills. It raises the quills at enemies. Then it runs backward into the enemies to poke them. Ouch!

Super Senses!

Honeybees carry balls of pollen back to their hives in patches of hair on their legs.

Q Why was everyone talking about the honeybees?

A They were making a buzz.

Some animals' senses are extremely sharp. A day before a storm, honeybees can feel tiny changes in the air. This tells them rain is coming. Before the storm hits, they gather lots of nectar to eat. That way, they won't have to go out in the rain for food.

Word Power

SENSES: The abilities of sight, smell, taste, hearing, and touch

A great gray owl listens for prey while it flies.

Great gray owls have amazing hearing. It helps them find prey. They can even hear rodents crawling under snow from the sky!

| Q | What does an owl say to answer the phone? | "Who-whooo is it?" | A |

western tarsier

Tarsiers (TAR-see-urs) are small mammals with giant eyes. They are nocturnal. Their huge eyes let them see in total darkness.

Word Power

NOCTURNAL: Active at night

Saving the Day!

Animals with amazing powers can help humans. Scientists studied a fly with special ears. They found it can pinpoint the location of a sound better than any other animal. Experts are using the structure of the fly's ears to make better hearing aids. Animal superpowers really *can* save the day!

Scientists are still studying how the fly picks out one sound—such as a cricket song—in a noisy setting.

QUIZ WHIZ

How much do you know about animal superpowers? After reading this book, probably a lot! Take this quiz and find out.

Answers are at the bottom of p. 31.

1 How long does it take a chameleon to grab an insect?
A. less than one second
B. five seconds
C. ten seconds
D. one minute

2 How do secretary birds knock out their prey?
A. with a bite
B. with a headbutt
C. with a kick
D. none of the above

3 Which animal can carry 50 times its own weight?
A. a fishing spider
B. a cuttlefish
C. a sea otter
D. a leafcutter ant

4 What do some tarantulas throw at enemies?
A. quills
B. spider silk
C. leg hairs
D. ants

5 Why are pygmy seahorses bumpy?
A. to blend in with coral
B. to lure in prey
C. to show off to mates
D. to scare enemies

6 When threatened, pufferfish swell up by _____.
A. gulping water
B. sucking in air
C. eating a big snack
D. all of the above

7 What do honeybees do if they feel rain coming?
A. buzz extra loud
B. gather lots of food
C. fly in circles
D. clean their hives

Answers: 1. A, 2. C, 3. D, 4. C, 5. A, 6. A, 7. B

GLOSSARY

CAMOUFLAGE: An animal's natural color or shape that blends in with its surroundings

NOCTURNAL: Active at night

PREDATOR: An animal that hunts and eats other animals

PREY: An animal that is eaten by another animal

SENSES: The abilities of sight, smell, taste, hearing, and touch

TEXTURE: The way a surface feels and looks